D1607152

FREEDOM'S PROMISE

THE INDIAN REMOVAL ACT
AND THE TRAIL OF TEARS

BY DUCHESS HARRIS, JD, PHD

WITH KATE CONLEY

Core Library

An Imprint of Abdo Publishing
abdobooks.com

Cover image: In the 1830s, Native Americans marched through snow when they were forced to move west.

abdobooks.com

Published by Abdo Publishing, a division of ABDO, PO Box 398166,
Minneapolis, Minnesota 55439. Copyright © 2020 by Abdo Consulting
Group, Inc. International copyrights reserved in all countries. No part of this
book may be reproduced in any form without written permission from the
publisher. Core Library™ is a trademark and logo of Abdo Publishing.

Printed in the United States of America, North Mankato, Minnesota
092019
012020

THIS BOOK CONTAINS
RECYCLED MATERIALS

Cover Photo: Al Moldvay/The Denver Post/Getty Images
Interior Photos: Al Moldvay/The Denver Post/Getty Images, 1; Picture History/Newscom, 5,
43; Nancy Carter/North Wind Picture Archives, 6–7; John T. Bowen/Circa Images/Newscom,
9; Jacquelyn Martin/AP Images, 12–13; Underwood Archives/UIG Universal Images Group/
Newscom, 14; Everett Collection/Newscom, 20–21; K. Cathey/Shutterstock Images, 24; Paul
Morigi/Smithsonian National Museum of the American Indian/AP Images, 26; Red Line Editorial,
28, 39; Jnix/Shutterstock Images, 30; Troy Anderson/NativeStock, 32–33; Ed Lallo/The LIFE Images
Collection/Getty Images, 34; Artsy Shot Photography/Shutterstock Images, 40

Editor: Maddie Spalding
Series Designer: Ryan Gale

Library of Congress Control Number: 2019942095

Publisher's Cataloging-in-Publication Data

Names: Harris, Duchess, author. | Conley, Kate, author.
Title: The indian removal act and the trail of tears / by Duchess Harris and Kate Conley
Description: Minneapolis, Minnesota : Abdo Publishing, 2020 | Series: Freedom's promise |
    Includes online resources and index.
Identifiers: ISBN 9781532190834 (lib. bdg.) | ISBN 9781532176685 (ebook)
Subjects: LCSH: United States. Indian Removal Act of 1830--Juvenile literature. | Trail of
    Tears, 1838-1839--Juvenile literature. | United States--Territorial expansion--Juvenile
    literature. | Cherokee Indian Removal, 1838-1839--Juvenile literature. | Indians of
    North America--Relocation--Juvenile literature. | Race discrimination--Juvenile
    literature.
Classification: DDC 975.004--dc23

CONTENTS

A LETTER FROM DUCHESS

In the early 1800s, white settlers oppressed Native people. This relationship of dominance is called settler colonialism. We can understand the Indian Removal Act through this concept. President Andrew Jackson signed this act into law in 1830. The act allowed the US government to offer land west of the Mississippi River to Native people in exchange for their lands. But the government often did not give Native people a choice. They forced Native Americans from their homelands. In 1838 more than 5,000 Cherokee Native Americans died on a march called the Trail of Tears.

This story is a narrative of resistance. After Native Americans were forcibly removed from their lands, they did everything they could to preserve their cultures. It is important to tell this story so people learn how discrimination hurts others. It helps us understand that it is important to respect the people and cultures around us. As you read this book, think of ways you can value people around you today, including those of different cultures.

Some images of the Trail of Tears show Cherokee traveling in wagons or on horses, but most were forced to walk.

STEALING NATIVE LANDS

I n 1829 thousands of Americans hoping to strike it rich moved to Georgia. Gold had just been discovered in the northern part of the state. The gold was on land that belonged to the Cherokee Nation.

The Cherokee's land was not part of the United States. The US government treated Native communities as independent nations. As independent nations, they were in control of their own lands. But white Americans mined gold on Cherokee land without permission.

The gold rush was one of many problems for Native peoples in the Southeast. For years,

In the 1800s, many Cherokee lived in log homes.

they had uneasy relationships with white people who settled around their lands. As the American population grew, the demand for land became greater. White Americans looked for more land to settle. Lands near established cities had already been purchased. So people began to buy land farther away from the cities. Eventually, all the available land was claimed. There were other fertile lands near white settlements. But these lands were not available to US citizens. They belonged to Native nations.

JOHN ROSS

John Ross served as chief of the Cherokee Nation for nearly 40 years. Ross was born in Turkeytown, Cherokee Territory, in 1790. Turkeytown was near present-day Centre, Alabama. His father was Scottish. His mother was part Cherokee. She raised Ross as a Cherokee. Ross led the Cherokee through decades of violence and upheaval. He tried to negotiate with government officials to protect the Cherokees' land rights. When the Cherokee were forced to resettle, Ross established their new government. He helped them survive and rebuild.

John Ross was the chief of the Cherokee Nation from 1828 to 1866.

FORCED REMOVAL

President Andrew Jackson encouraged the US Congress to pass the Indian Removal Act. Jackson signed the act into law in May 1830. The act allowed Jackson to give unsettled land west of the Mississippi River to Native peoples in exchange for their lands east of the river.

Under the act, Native Americans were supposed to be able to choose whether to exchange their lands. But in reality, the US government did not give Native Americans a choice. US troops forced thousands of

Native Americans from their homes. The Cherokee were among those who were forced to leave. The troops threatened people who refused to leave with violence. They ordered Native Americans to march to the new land under harsh conditions. The journey was difficult. Thousands of people died along the way. For this reason, the Cherokee call this journey the Trail of Tears.

The Indian Removal Act left deep scars on the people who were forced to move.

PERSPECTIVES

VOICES OF OPPOSITION

Andrew Jackson strongly supported the idea of Indian removal. So did many Americans who wanted land. But not all Americans thought it was a good idea. Many spoke out against the act. They argued that it went against the American ideal of freedom. They believed it violated Native people's civil rights. Congress members were also divided on the idea. The act passed in the US Senate in April 1830 by nine votes. The House of Representatives voted on the act one month later. The act passed in the House by only six votes.

Families were separated. The survival of the Native peoples and their cultures seemed uncertain. Native Americans had to learn to live on strange land far from what they knew.

But the period of Indian removal is also a story of strength. Communities rose up and rebuilt themselves. It took many years, and it was not easy. One of the largest Native communities today is the Cherokee Nation. Approximately 360,000 people belong to the Cherokee Nation. This makes it the largest tribal nation in the United States. The Cherokee are committed to preserving their traditional culture and values.

EXPLORE ONLINE

Chapter One introduces you to the Cherokee Nation and the Trail of Tears. The video at the website below goes into more depth on these topics. Does the video answer any of the questions you had about what life was like for the Cherokee during this period? What new information did you learn?

THE CHEROKEE NATION: NEW ECHOTA
abdocorelibrary.com/indian-removal-act

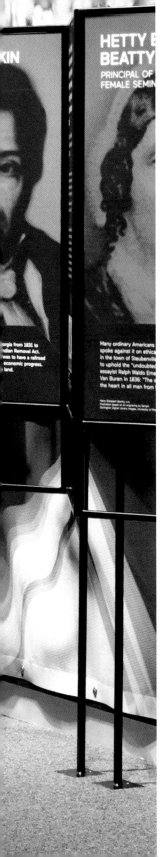

THE ROAD TO REMOVAL

I n the 1790s, politicians began talking about the "Indian Problem." They were referring to a dispute about land ownership. Government leaders wanted to provide white settlers with new lands. But Native nations owned much of the land settlers wanted.

President George Washington and other leaders came up with a plan. They called it the "civilization plan." Federal agents encouraged Native Americans to adopt the cultures and traditions of white settlers. White Americans thought their way of life was civilized. They believed Native Americans could only become

The Smithsonian's National Museum of the American Indian in Washington, DC, shares the story of the Trail of Tears and the Indian Removal Act.

Throughout the 1800s, relationships between Native and white Americans were often tense.

civilized by adopting their practices. But Native communities had existed long before the settlers came. They had their own civilizations and practices. Federal agents wanted to erase their Native identities.

THE CIVILIZATION PLAN

Federal agents taught Native Americans to farm the way white settlers did. They hoped Native Americans would begin to rely more on farming and less on hunting. The Native American tradition of hunting required vast tracts of land. Officials thought Native Americans would not need as much land if they gave up hunting. They hoped Native American farmers would willingly sell their hunting lands to the US government.

Some Native nations quickly adopted European practices. Those who did so in the Southeast became known as the Five Civilized Tribes. The Cherokee, Choctaw, Chickasaw, Seminole, and Muscogee nations made up this group. White settlers called the Muscogee the Creek.

THE LOUISIANA PURCHASE

The United States expanded in the early 1800s. Under President Thomas Jefferson, the US government completed the Louisiana Purchase

ADOPTING SETTLER TRADITIONS

The Cherokee Nation adopted many aspects of white settler culture. They picked out the parts that would benefit their communities. For example, the Cherokee Nation created a constitution. Its constitution was its governing document. It was based on the US Constitution. Also, a Cherokee man named Sequoyah learned about written language from white settlers. Traditionally, the Cherokee did not have a written language. Sequoyah created a Cherokee alphabet. It was easy to learn. Most Cherokee quickly learned to read.

in 1803. The government bought land from France. This land was west of the Mississippi River. The United States doubled in size with this land purchase. Native Americans, Africans, and Europeans already lived on this land. Soon white Americans settled on this land as well.

Jefferson wanted to move Native Americans from the Southeast into this new territory. Land in the Southeast was desirable. It had rich soil and was good for farming. White Americans wanted to plant cotton on this land. Cotton was a valuable crop.

Under federal law, Native nations were independent. They were in charge of their own decisions, laws, and governments. This affected land deals. Federal law required a treaty between both parties to sell land. Some Muscogee, Cherokee, and Choctaws signed treaties with the US government in the early 1800s. They agreed to move west of the Mississippi River. But most Native American nations did not sign treaties. They did not want to move to a strange territory.

A VIOLENT CONFLICT

Distrust grew between nations that accepted deals and those that did not. Even within nations, some members were allied with white settlers while others were not. This was the case with the Muscogee Nation. On August 30, 1813, approximately 700 Muscogee took up arms against white settlers and their Muscogee allies. They attacked Fort Mims near present-day

PERSPECTIVES

WHY AGREE TO A TREATY?

Some Native American nations agreed to give up part of their lands. This was not an easy choice. But many felt it was the safest course of action. They hoped white settlers would leave them alone if they gave up some of their lands. But this strategy did not work. The population of white settlers grew. They sought out more lands. They illegally moved to some Native peoples' lands. Settlers burned Native Americans' houses and stole their livestock. Others attacked or even killed Native Americans.

Stockton, Alabama. Enslaved Africans were in the fort as well. The group of Muscogee killed approximately 250 people. This attack became known as the Fort Mims Massacre. It led to a conflict called the Creek War.

After the massacre, the US government sent approximately 3,000 soldiers to Alabama. General Andrew Jackson led the troops. On March 27, 1814, US troops defeated the Muscogee at the Battle of Horseshoe Bend. They killed more than 800 Muscogee warriors. They took 500 Muscogee women and children as hostages.

The Muscogee surrendered after the battle. The war ended. The Muscogee were forced to give up 23 million acres (9.3 million ha) of their lands. Between 1814 and 1824, the US government gained land as the Muscogee and other nations signed treaties or were forced to move. This new land included parts of seven states and territories: Alabama, Florida, Georgia, Tennessee, Mississippi, Kentucky, and North Carolina.

STRAIGHT TO THE
SOURCE

In February 1803, Thomas Jefferson wrote a letter to Benjamin Hawkins. Hawkins was a federal agent. His job was to negotiate with Native American nations on behalf of the US government. In his letter to Hawkins, Jefferson wrote:

> *I consider the business of hunting as already become insufficient to furnish clothing and subsistence to the Indians. The promotion of agriculture, therefore, and household manufacture, are essential in their preservation. . . . This will enable them to live on much smaller portions of land. . . . While they are learning to do better on less land, our increasing numbers will be calling for more land. . . . This commerce, then, will be for the good of both, and those who are friends to both ought to encourage it.*

> Source: Thomas Jefferson. *The Essential Jefferson.* Indianapolis, IN: Hackett Publishing, 2006. 201.

Point of View

Why did Jefferson think the civilization plan would be good for both settlers and Native Americans? Read back through this chapter. Do you think Native people's view of the plan was different than Jefferson's? Why or why not?

THE ACT AND ITS EFFECTS

A ndrew Jackson's military successes had brought him national attention. He ran for president in 1828 and won the election. As president, he supported the idea of removing Native Americans from their lands. Under his leadership, Congress passed the Indian Removal Act. The act became law on May 28, 1830.

Jackson appointed commissioners. The commissioners met with tribes that lived east of the Mississippi River. They tried to get the tribes to sign treaties. The treaties would allow the government to exchange land east

Andrew Jackson, *left*, forced Native American leaders such as Muscogee chief Red Eagle, *right*, to sign treaties that took away tribal lands.

of the river for land west of the river. The government called the land west of the river Indian Territory. Commissioners could forcibly remove tribes that refused to agree to a treaty. Native Americans who already lived in Indian Territory had to make room for incoming Native Americans.

The US government and the Choctaw Nation signed the first treaty under the Indian Removal Act. It was called the Treaty of Dancing Rabbit Creek. The Choctaw lived in Mississippi, Alabama, Louisiana, and Florida. They had already given up much of their lands to the government. They signed the Treaty of Dancing Rabbit Creek in September 1830. They gave up another 11 million acres (4 million ha) of their land. Approximately 13,000 Choctaw left their homelands and moved to Indian Territory over the next few years.

The Choctaw removal was peaceful. But this was not the always the case. In 1833 the US government pressured the Seminoles to sign a treaty. The Seminoles lived in Florida. The government wanted them to move west. The terms of the treaty were unclear. Seminole chiefs signed the treaty. They did not think signing it meant they would have to leave their homelands.

The Seminoles refused to leave. Some fought back. This resulted in a conflict called the Second Seminole War. This war lasted from 1835 to 1842. US troops forced approximately 3,000 Seminoles to move to Indian Territory. Few Seminoles remained in Florida after the war. US troops later waged another war against

INDIAN TERRITORY

The Indian Nonintercourse Act helped define Indian Territory. The act was a series of measures passed between 1790 and 1847. It said that Native Americans could only sell their lands to the US government. The act defined Indian Territory as the area west of the Mississippi River that was not within the states of Missouri or Louisiana. Indian Territory also did not include the Arkansas territory. It was soon reduced to the present-day state of Oklahoma.

The Seminoles lived in thatched huts and learned how to survive in Florida's swamplands.

these Seminoles. Even after years of conflict, a group of Seminoles managed to survive. They hid in Florida.

THE CHEROKEE

Like the Muscogee, the Cherokee were divided over whether to leave their homelands. Some Cherokee resisted removal. They called themselves the National Party. John Ross led this group. Ross was the chief of the Cherokee Nation. Those in favor of signing a treaty called themselves the Treaty Party. Major Ridge led this group. The Treaty Party believed US troops would kill many Cherokee if they tried to resist. They thought removal was inevitable.

Ross met with President Jackson in January 1835. Ross said the Cherokee would only agree to a land deal for $20 million. He knew the US government would never give them that much money. Jackson returned with an offer of $5 million. Ross promised to take the offer back to the Cherokee Nation for a vote. But Jackson was tired of waiting. He sent an agent to talk with Ridge about the offer instead.

Ridge and the agent met at the Cherokee village of New Echota, Georgia. Ridge and a group of other Cherokee accepted Jackson's offer on December 29, 1835. The US government would pay the Cherokee Nation $5 million for their land. But there was a problem: Ridge did not have the authority to approve

Today, the Treaty of New Echota that Major Ridge and other Cherokee signed is on display at the National Museum of the American Indian.

the treaty. He was not a chief. He also did not have many supporters. Most of the Cherokee people did not want to sign a treaty.

The National Party opposed the treaty. More than 16,000 Cherokee signed a petition against it. They tried to fight it in the federal courts. Despite these efforts,

Congress approved the treaty in March 1836. It was called the Treaty of New Echota. Many Cherokee did not comply with the treaty. They refused to leave their homelands. By 1838 only 2,000 Cherokee had left. The US government sent General Winfield Scott and his troops to remove the Cherokee from their homelands.

THE TRAIL OF TEARS

On May 23, 1838, Scott ordered his 7,000 soldiers to round up

REMOVAL
ROUTES

The map below shows the routes of the five Native nations that were forced to leave their homes. How does this map help you better understand their journeys?

ARKANSAS TERRITORY

MISSOURI

KENTUCKY

VIRGINIA

INDIAN TERRITORY

TENNESSEE

NORTH CAROLINA

SOUTH CAROLINA

MISSISSIPPI

ALABAMA

GEORGIA

LOUISIANA

Mississippi River

ATLANTIC OCEAN

GULF OF MEXICO

FLORIDA TERRITORY

N W E S

Cherokee
Muscogee
Chickasaw
Seminole
Choctaw

the remaining Cherokee people. Everyone had to leave immediately. Soldiers forced the Cherokee into camps. The Cherokee waited there until the roundup was complete. Conditions in the camps were poor. Summer heat made the camps uncomfortable. Diseases spread quickly. Many Cherokee died.

In the fall of 1838, troops marched the Cherokee out of the camps. They set out in 13 groups called detachments. They headed toward Indian Territory.

Each detachment had approximately 1,000 people. The Cherokee made the 1,200-mile (1,900-km) journey on foot. They walked in driving rain, wind, and snow. The troops did not give them much food. The Cherokee did not have warm clothing. They were exposed to the brutal winter weather. The detachments did not stop to wait for the sick to rest and recover.

The detachments finally arrived in Indian Territory after 116 days of walking. Many people did not survive the journey. More than 5,000 Cherokee died

A statue in Pulaski, Tennessee, depicts a Cherokee family walking on the Trail of Tears. Pulaski is along the Trail of Tears route.

along the way. This was one-quarter of the entire Cherokee Nation. But the difficult days were not over. The Cherokee faced a new challenge. They had to rebuild their nation in a strange land.

STRAIGHT TO THE
SOURCE

Major Ridge faced criticism for signing the Treaty of New Echota. But he defended his position. He said:

We obtained the land from the living God above. [The Americans] got their title from the British. Yet they are strong and we are weak. We are few, they are many. We cannot remain here in safety and comfort. . . . We can never forget these homes, I know, but an unbending, iron necessity tells us we must leave them. I would willingly die to preserve them, but any forcible effort to keep them will cost us our lands, our lives and the lives of our children.

Source: John Ehle. *Trail of Tears: The Rise and Fall of the Cherokee Nation*. New York: Doubleday, 1988. 294.

What's the Big Idea?

Take a close look at this passage. How does Ridge describe the Cherokee's connection to their homelands? How does he summarize the conflict over whether to leave or remain on their lands?

LEGACY

B etween 1830 and 1840, the Indian Removal Act forced nearly 100,000 Native Americans to migrate to Indian Territory. Approximately 15,000 Native Americans died on this journey. The journey devastated the survivors. They arrived in Indian Territory exhausted, ill, and grieving. Their first year in the territory was one of transition. They had to build homes, plant crops, and establish local governments.

The US government promised support and supplies. It sent vendors to sell food in Indian Territory. But the process often did not run smoothly. Many times, the vendors arrived only once every other month. Many of the vendors

The Choctaws began their march to Indian Territory in the winter of 1830.

A group of Native Americans traveled along the Trail of Tears route in 1988 to remember those who suffered and died on the journey.

tried to cheat the Native Americans. Fresh meat was often expensive and of poor quality.

Many Native Americans tried to farm the land. But they had been forced to leave behind their livestock and farming tools. Without tools to till the soil, they had to do the work by hand. As a result, they planted their crops shallowly. The crops often dried out in the hot summer weather. Some people planted along streams as they had in their homelands. But these streams often flooded and washed away the crops.

Another challenge the Cherokee faced was divisions within their nation. The Cherokee had arrived in Indian Territory in different waves. The first wave had signed treaties in the 1810s and 1820s. These Cherokee had established their own government. They had their own chief. Many of them did not welcome new arrivals. They did not want other Cherokee to disrupt their established lives and government. Other disagreements also arose among the Cherokee. The US government had offered the Cherokee $5 million for their land in the Treaty of New Echota. But Ross and his followers had not signed the treaty. They had been forced to move but were not paid for their land. These tensions were finally resolved in 1846 when the Cherokee groups signed a treaty. The treaty united the Cherokee.

THE OKLAHOMA TERRITORY

Gradually, peace and order settled upon the Native peoples living in Indian Territory. Native nations formed their own governments. People built homes and learned to live on the new land.

This peace was short-lived. In the 1870s, white Americans discovered oil in Indian Territory. Some people wanted to build railroads into the territory. They pressured Congress to open this area to white settlement.

In 1889 Congress opened 3,100 acres (1,250 ha) of land in the western part of Indian Territory. This land had not been assigned to any Native nation. It was made available to white settlers. This area was called Oklahoma Territory.

Four years later, the US government opened up the

THE DAWES ACT

In 1887 Congress passed the Dawes Act. Before this time, Native nations had owned lands as communities. These lands were called reservations. Under the Dawes Act, the government offered land to individual Native Americans. The land they received was called an allotment. A typical allotment was 160 acres (65 ha). Native Americans had to become US citizens to receive allotments. As more people took advantage of this offer, reservations grew smaller. Today, the Cherokee Nation owns only 2 percent of the land it originally had before the allotments.

remaining parts of Indian Territory for white settlement. Then in 1907, Oklahoma became a state. The lands owned by Native nations became reservations within the state.

EFFECTS

Today, more than 30 Native American tribes live in Oklahoma. There are no longer reservations in the state. Most Native Americans in Oklahoma live in the eastern part of the state.

Though the Indian Removal Act was passed more than 150 years ago, its effects can be seen in Native communities today. The US government's oppression of Native peoples resulted in a loss of some parts of Native cultures. It also created poverty within Native communities. This poverty persists today.

Generations of Native Americans faced hardships during and after the removal period. This period of US history remained overlooked for decades. But over time, more people learned about it. In 1987 Congress established the Trail of Tears National Historic Trail. It is 5,043 miles (8,114 km) long. It follows the Cherokee's removal routes. It crosses through parts of nine states. It reminds people of the Native Americans who died on the Trail of Tears.

In 2009 the US Senate passed a resolution. The resolution was an apology to all Native Americans. It recognized the mistreatment Native Americans endured under years of US policies. Some Native Americans applauded the effort.

POVERTY
RATES

The Indian Removal Act pushed many Native Americans into poverty. Today, the poverty rate is still high in many Native communities. This graph compares the poverty rates among Native Americans to the overall US poverty rates in recent years. How do these rates differ? How do you think the historic mistreatment of Native Americans influences these poverty rates?

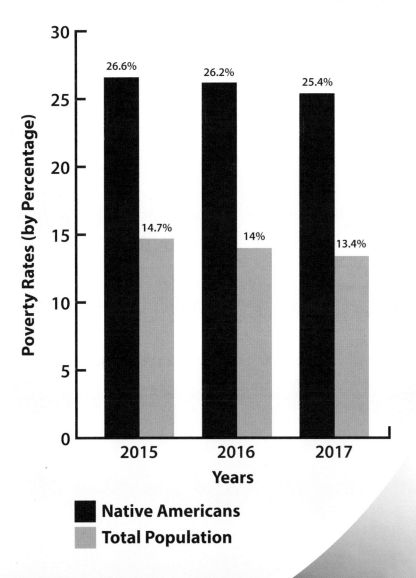

For others, words were not enough to ease the pain of losing their homelands.

The apology looked to the future. It expressed a hope that all Americans could one day live together in peace. It will still take many years to repair the damages caused by the Indian Removal Act. But the apology could be a step toward a more promising future.

FURTHER EVIDENCE

Chapter Four covers the legacy of the Indian Removal Act. What was one of the main points of the chapter? What evidence is included to support this point? Read the article at the website below. Does the information from the article support this point? Or does it offer a new piece of evidence?

AMERICAN INDIAN REMOVAL
abdocorelibrary.com/indian-removal-act

Today, Native Americans continue to keep their traditions alive through festivals and celebrations.

FAST FACTS

- Congress passed the Indian Removal Act in 1830. Under this act, US troops forced Native Americans living east of the Mississippi River to move west of the river. The lands the US government set aside for Native American settlement were known as Indian Territory.

- Approximately 100,000 Native Americans were forced to move to Indian Territory. The Native nations most affected by the Indian Removal Act were the Cherokee, Muscogee, Choctaw, Chickasaw, and Seminole nations.

- In 1835 some Cherokee signed the Treaty of New Echota. The treaty gave the Cherokee's lands to the US government. Some Cherokee opposed the treaty. But all were forced to move to Indian Territory. More than 5,000 Cherokee died on this forced march. The march is known as the Trail of Tears.

- In 1987 Congress established the Trail of Tears National Historic Trail. It reminds people of the Native Americans who died on the Trail of Tears.

- In 2009 Congress formally apologized to Native Americans for how the US government had mistreated them.

STOP AND THINK

Tell the Tale

Chapter Four describes how Native Americans formed settlements in Indian Territory in the 1830s. Imagine you are visiting Indian Territory at the time. Write 200 words about what you see. Describe the struggles you see as the Native Americans adapt to living in a new place.

Dig Deeper

After reading this book, what questions do you still have about the Indian Removal Act and the Trail of Tears? With an adult's help, find a few reliable sources that can help you answer your questions. Write a short paragraph about what you learned.

Why Do I Care?

You may not have a connection to a Native American nation. But that doesn't mean you can't think about the legacy of the Indian Removal Act. How did this act shape Native American communities today? How might your community or other communities be different if the act had not passed?

GLOSSARY

allies
groups of people who partner with and support each other

civilized
considered developed and educated

fertile
able to produce many crops or plants

massacre
the killing of many people

oppression
the unjust use of power over a group of people

petition
a formal written request

reservation
land in the United States that has been set aside for Native Americans to live on

resolution
in law, something that is passed by legislative bodies that is often a statement of policy or belief

subsistence
something that is needed to survive, such as food and water

treaty
a formal written agreement between nations

vendor
someone who sells goods and services

ONLINE RESOURCES

To learn more about the Indian Removal Act and the Trail of Tears, visit our free resource websites below.

Visit **abdocorelibrary.com** or scan this QR code for free Common Core resources for teachers and students, including vetted activities, multimedia, and booklinks, for deeper subject comprehension.

Visit **abdobooklinks.com** or scan this QR code for free additional online weblinks for further learning. These links are routinely monitored and updated to provide the most current information available.

LEARN MORE

Mooney, Carla. *Traditional Stories of the Southeast Nations.* Minneapolis, MN: Abdo Publishing, 2018.

Rea, Amy C. *The Trail of Tears.* Minneapolis, MN: Abdo Publishing, 2017.

ABOUT THE
AUTHORS

Duchess Harris, JD, PhD

Dr. Harris is a professor of American Studies at Macalester College and curator of the Duchess Harris Collection of ABDO books. She is also the coauthor of the titles in the collection, which features popular selections such as *Hidden Human Computers: The Black Women of NASA* and series including News Literacy and Being Female in America.

Before working with ABDO, Dr. Harris authored several other books on the topics of race, culture, and American history. She served as an associate editor for *Litigation News*, the American Bar Association Section of Litigation's quarterly flagship publication, and was the first editor in chief of *Law Raza*, an interactive online journal covering race and the law, published at William Mitchell College of Law. She has earned a PhD in American Studies from the University of Minnesota and a JD from William Mitchell College of Law.

Kate Conley

Kate Conley has been writing nonfiction books for children for more than ten years. When she's not writing, Conley spends her time reading, sewing, and solving crossword puzzles. She lives in Minnesota with her husband and two children.

INDEX